GW01117164

God is...

The Bible Tells Me So Press

God Is...

A children's book produced
by The Bible Tells Me So Press

Copyright © 2018
The Bible Tells Me So Corporation

All rights reserved. No part of this book, neither text nor illustrations, may be reproduced or stored in any form or by any electronic or mechanical means without permission in writing by the publisher.

PUBLISHED BY
THE BIBLE TELLS ME SO CORPORATION
2111 CRESCENT AVE, SUITE C ANAHEIM, CA 92801
WWW.THEBIBLETELLSMESO.COM

First Printing Februrary, 2018

God

is...

big.

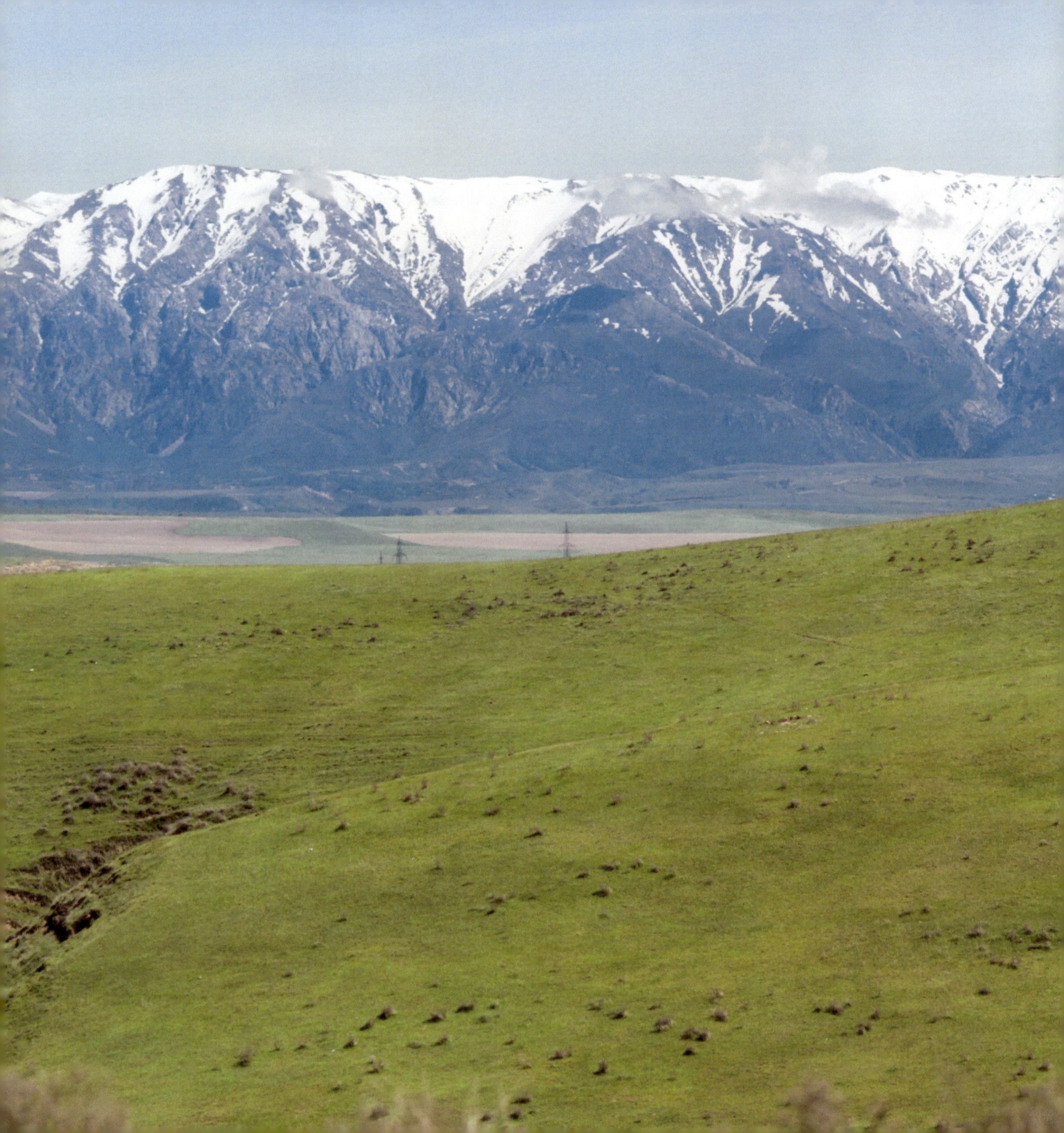

Very, very,

BIG!

God is bigger than

all the animals.

God is bigger than

everything!

God is the biggest

of all!

God

is...

strong

and mighty.

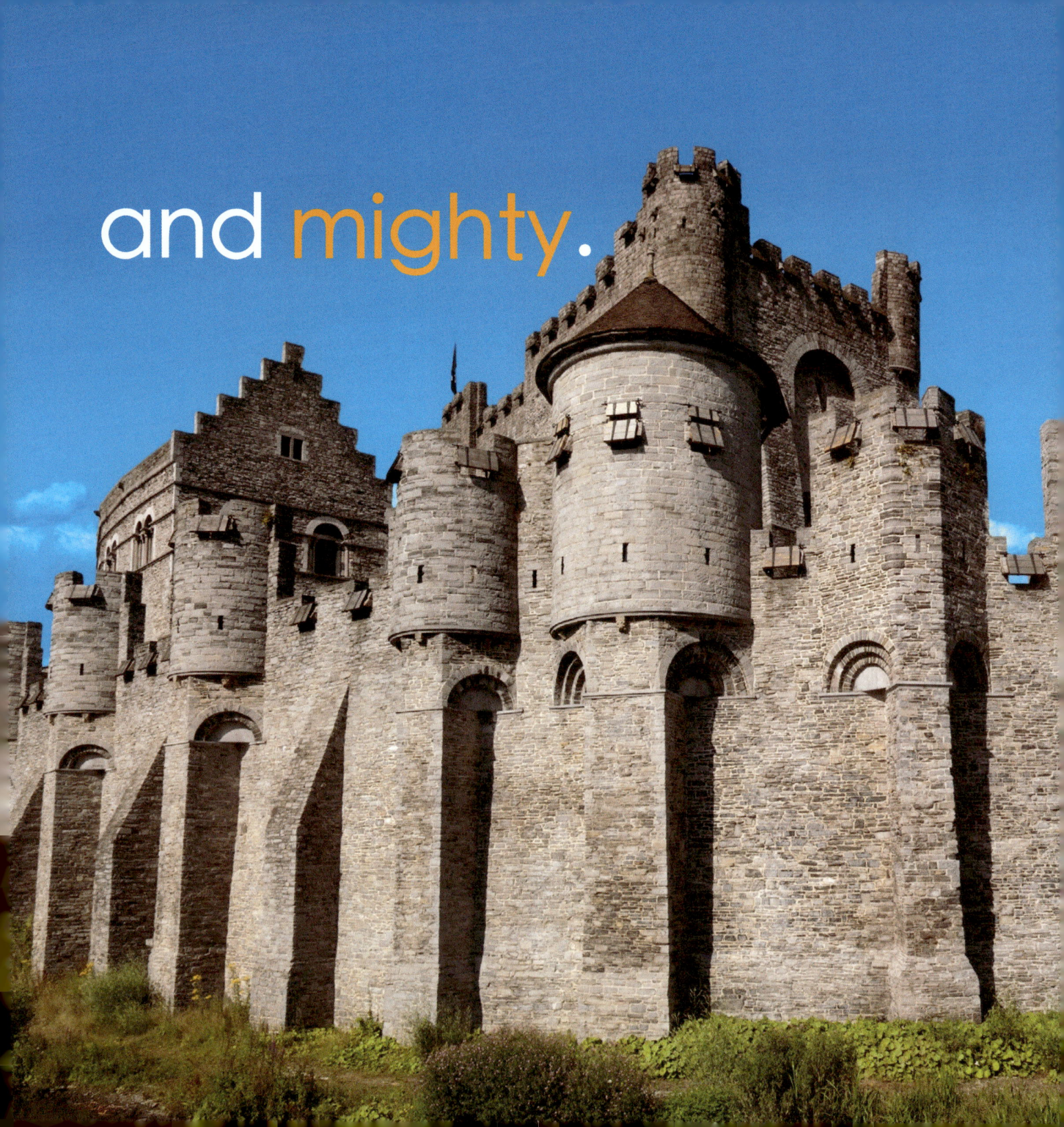

God is **stronger** than the mountains.

Nothing is **stronger** and **mightier** than God!

God is the strongest and mightiest

of **all!**

God

is...

kind.

He gives little bees
plenty of flowers.

He gives the birds

beautiful
feathers.

He gives animals fur

to keep them warm
in the cold.

God

is...

love.

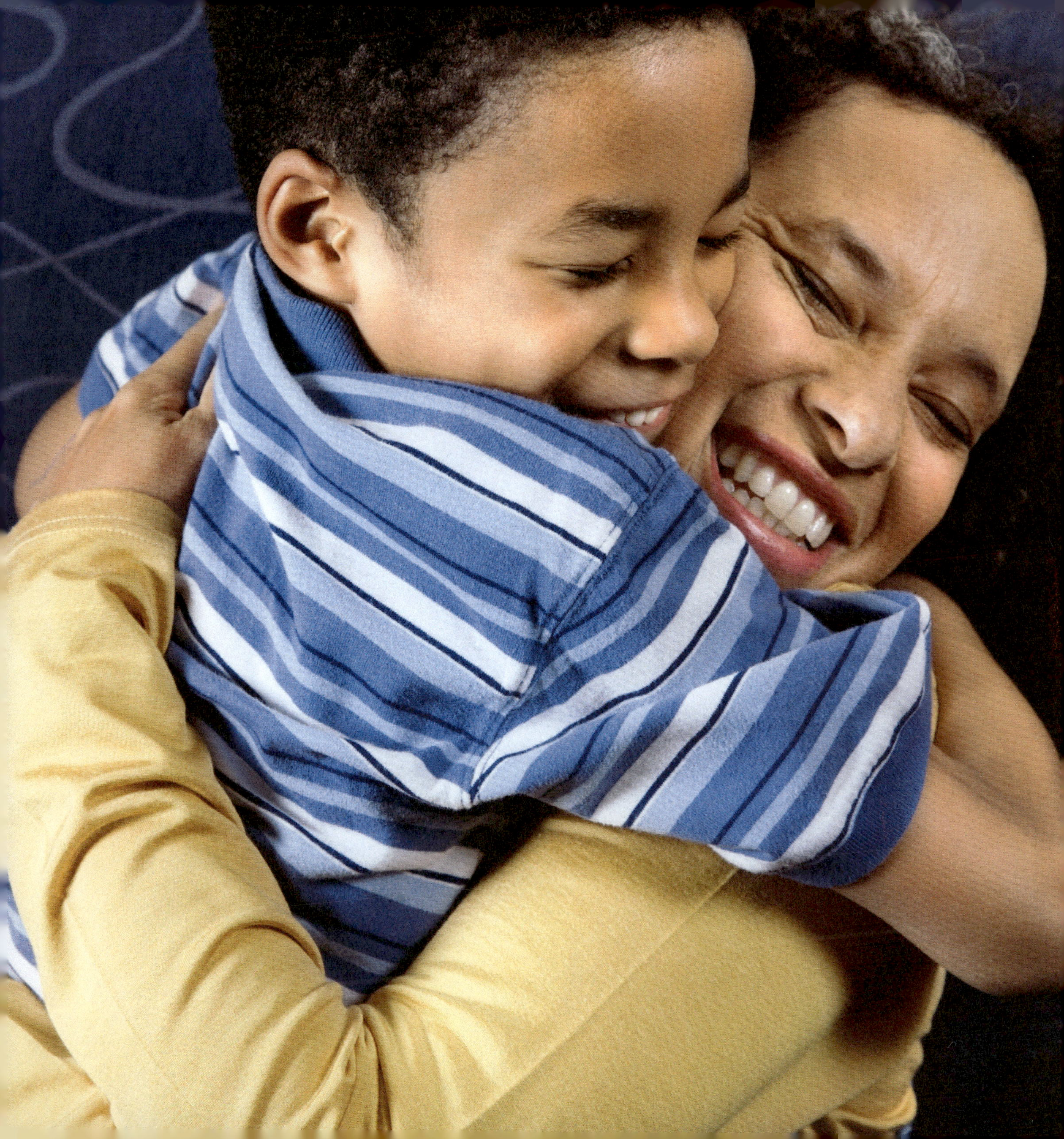

God
loves
you

and
me.

No matter what
you look like

or where you are from,

God loves everyone

very much!

God

is...

always bright
and shining.

There is no darkness **at all** in God.

Because
God is *light*.

God is
many wonderful
things.

He is...

big,

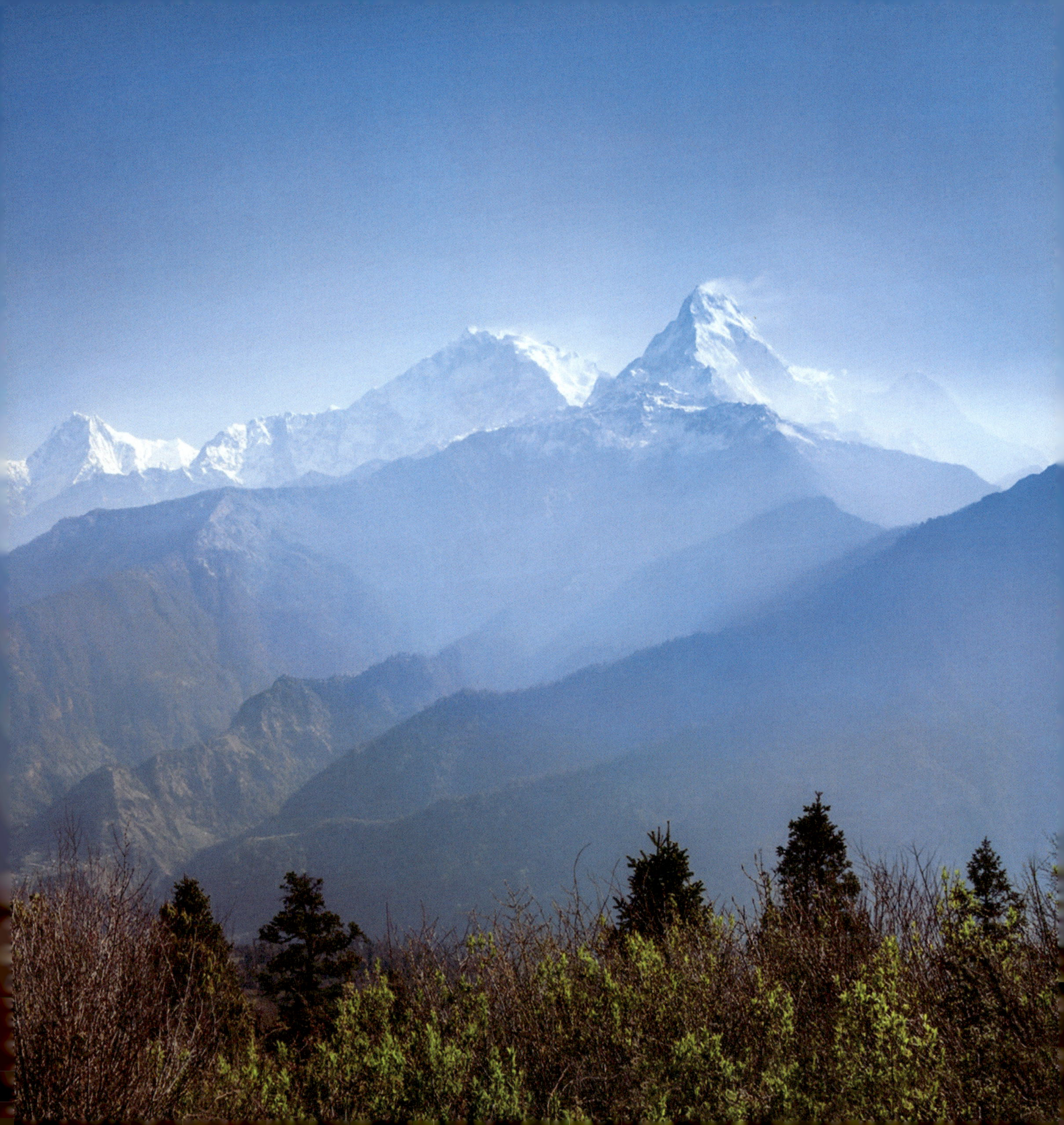

strong,

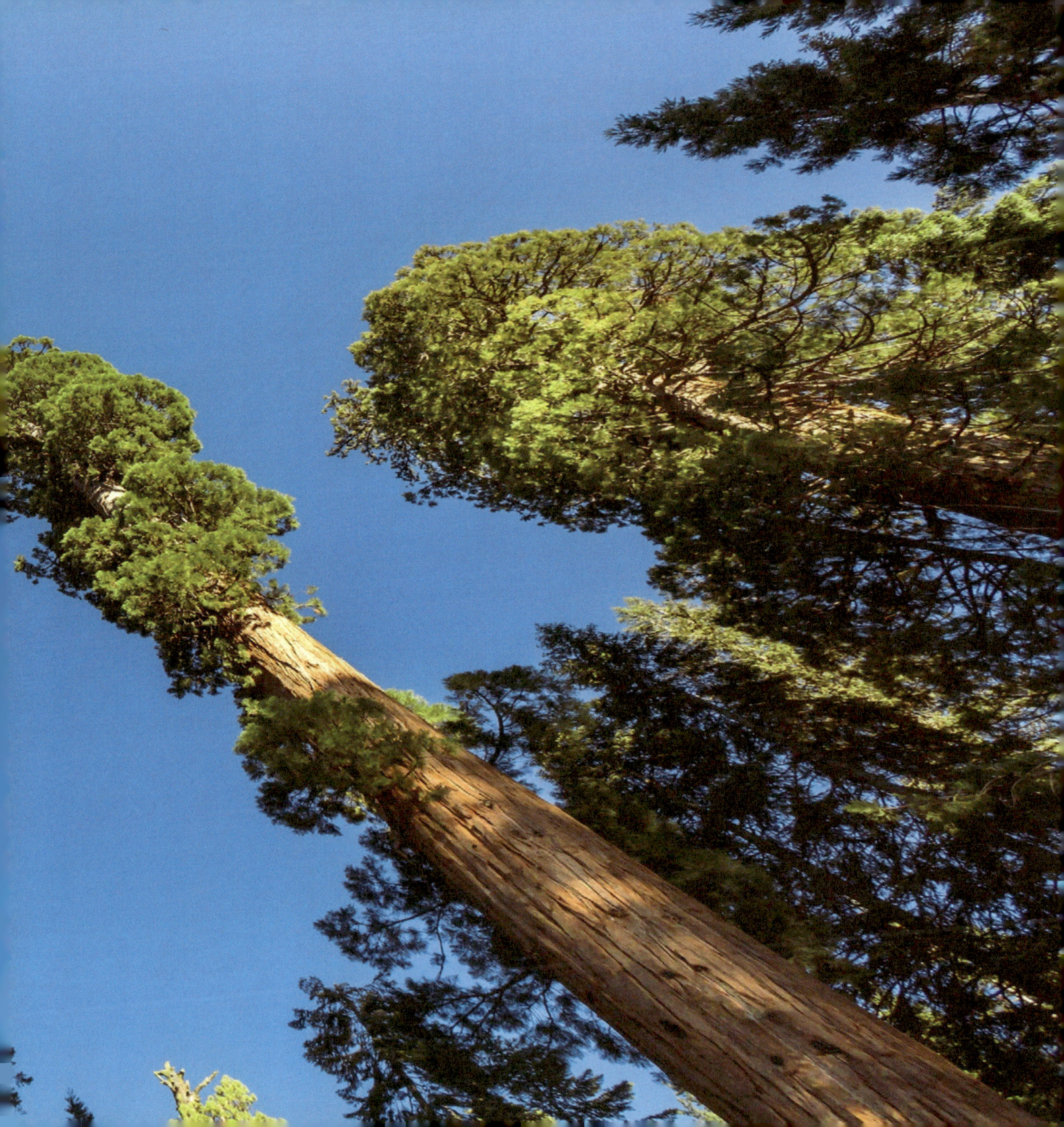

mighty,

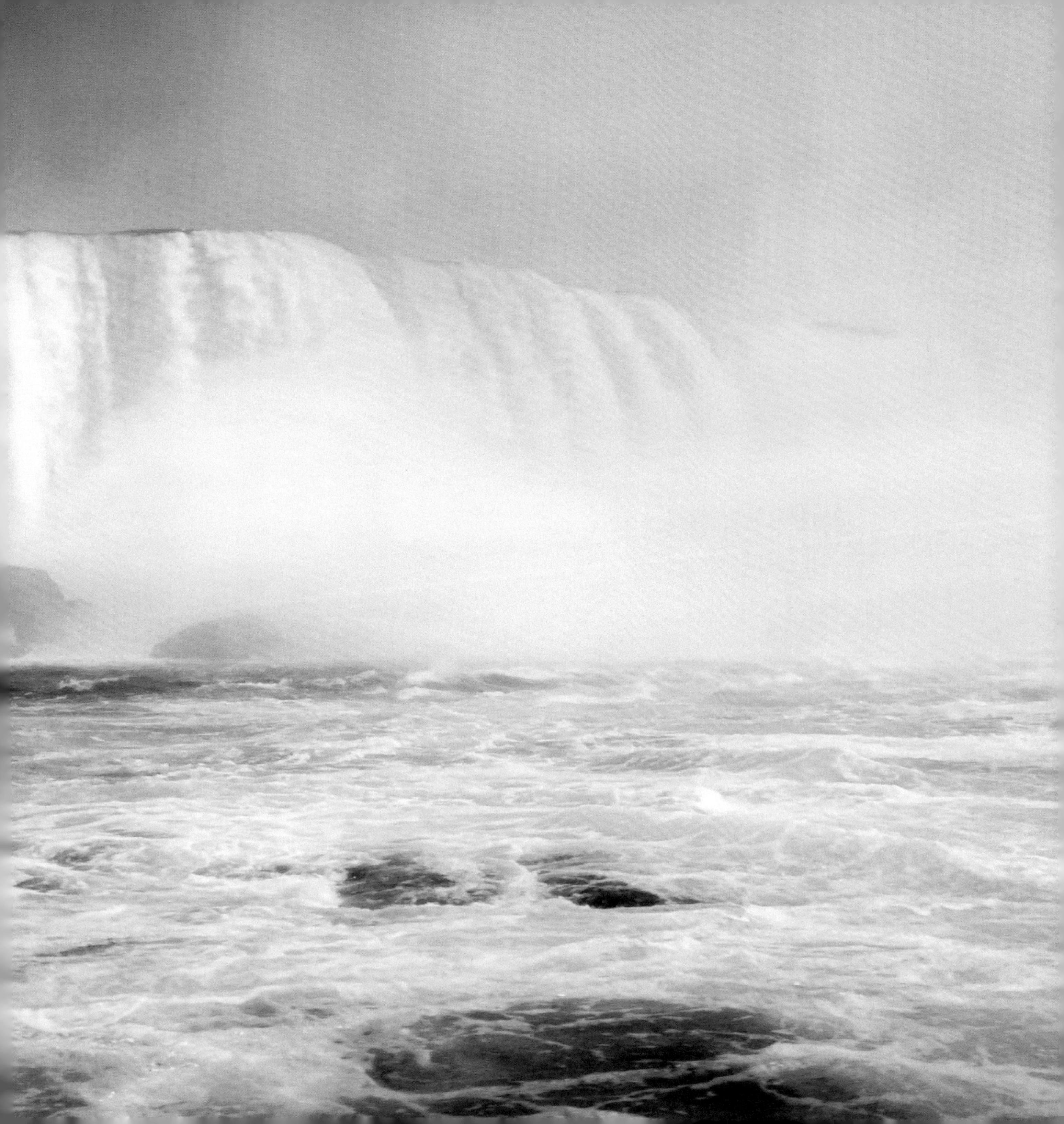

kind,

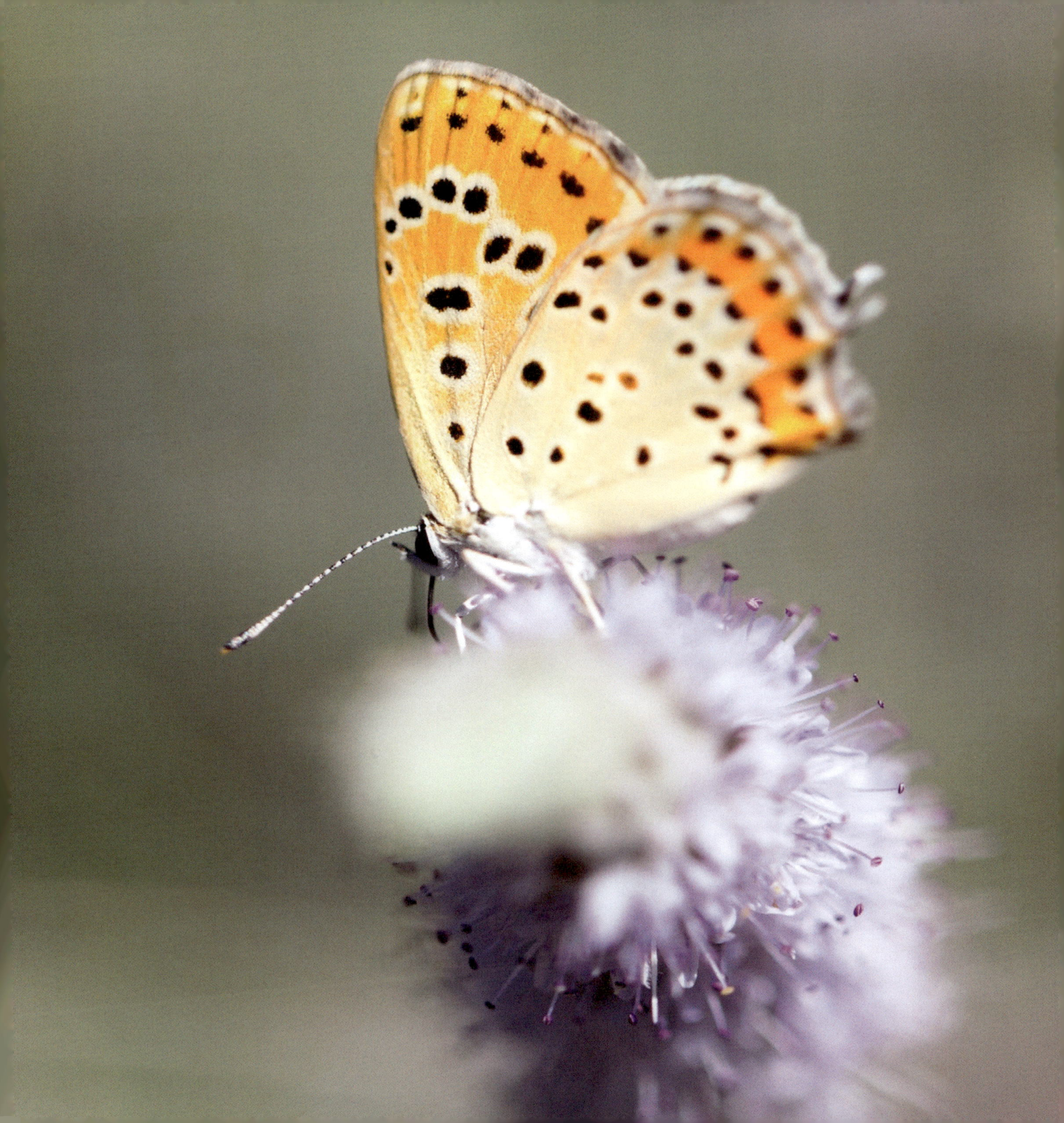

love,

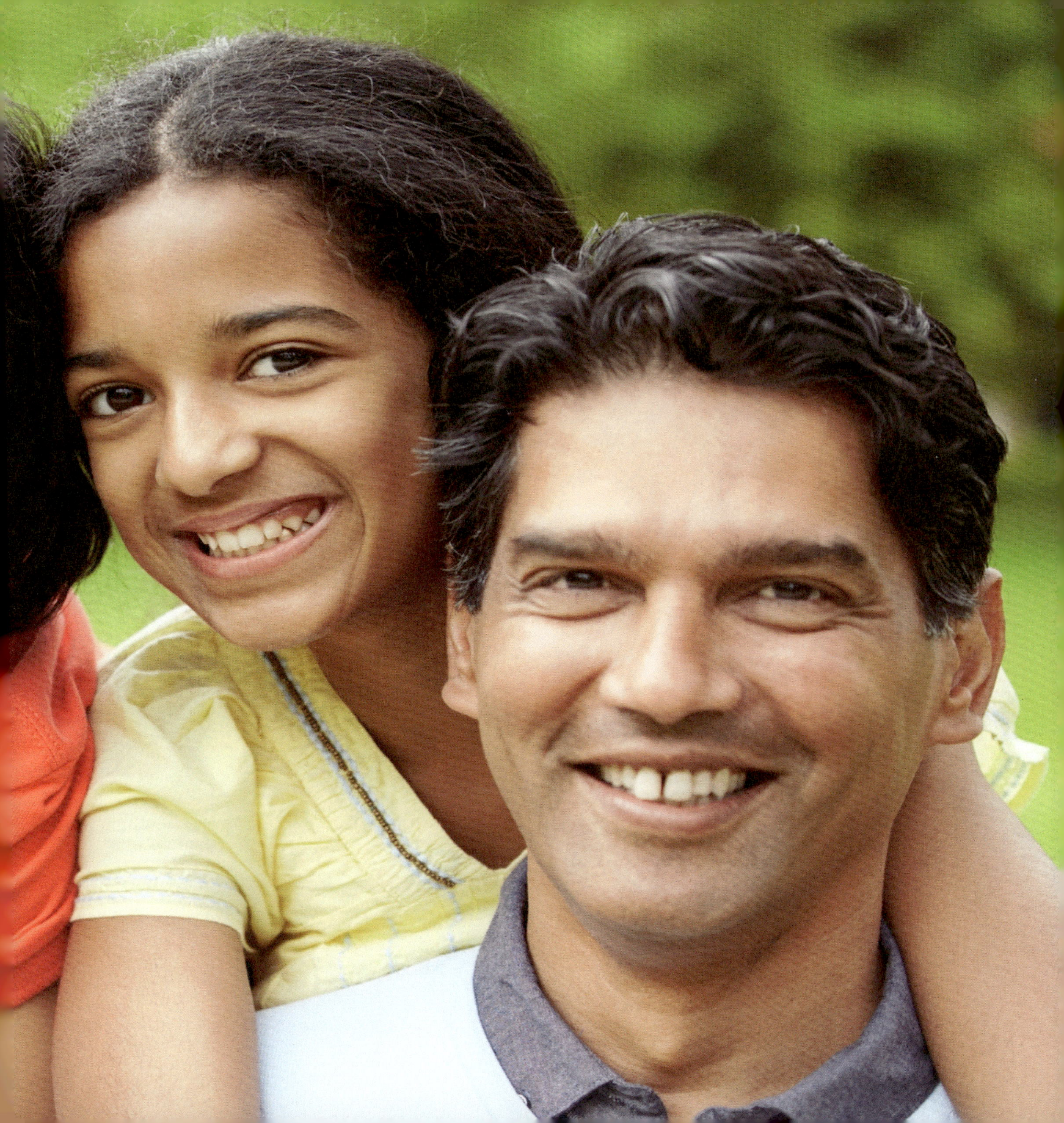

and light.

For more
books, videos, songs, and crafts
visit us online at
TheBibleTellsMeSo.com

Standing on the Bible and growing!

Printed in Great Britain
by Amazon